I0192105

CHASE NORDMAN

Responding to Parents (for Teachers)

Real Responses to the Real Things Parents Say

First published by Hallway Press 2025

Copyright © 2025 by Chase Nordman

All rights reserved. No part of this publication may be reproduced, stored or transmitted in any form or by any means, electronic, mechanical, photocopying, recording, scanning, or otherwise without written permission from the publisher. It is illegal to copy this book, post it to a website, or distribute it by any other means without permission.

First edition

ISBN: 979-8-9994238-2-5

This book was professionally typeset on Reedsy.
Find out more at reedsy.com

For my parents

Contents

II Behavior and Discipline

III   Academic Pressure and Grade Concerns

IV Mental, Medical, & Emotional Concerns

V Family, Home, or Custody Issues

XV   Templates for Contact

XVI   Power Phrases

XVII   Final Words and Acknowledgments

Why this book exists

If you've ever walked out of a parent conversation thinking, *"That could have gone better,"* you're not the only one. As educators, we're trained to manage classrooms, plan lessons, and meet standards, but almost no one shows us how to talk to parents. And somehow, those conversations end up being some of the most important ones we have all year.

Parents aren't the problem. Most of them care deeply and want to help. But that partnership can get real messy real fast. Some parents come in defensively. Some just want to be their kid's best friend. Some contact us too much. Some don't respond at all. And what we say in each of those moments can either build trust or shut it down.

This book was made to make those moments easier.

Not scripted. Not fake. Just clear, calm, and professional language that keeps things on track when emotions start running high, for teachers AND parents.

Responding to Parents (for Teachers) is full of real examples, parent statements, archetypes, quick communication templates, and ready to use phrases you can actually use. Whether it's a quick chat in the lobby or a tense conference you've had scheduled for a week, you'll find the words that help you stay grounded and keep the focus on the student where it belongs.

How to use this book

Each page in *Responding to Parents (for Teachers)* starts with a real situation teachers face, like a tricky email, a concerning voicemail, a tense conference, or a moment that could go sideways fast.

Below each one, you'll find a suggested response (**You say**) written to be calm, clear, and professional without sounding scripted. Then comes the **Why it works** section, so you can understand the thinking behind the words and make them sound like *you*.

This book **is not a script**. It's a toolkit.

Use it as a guide, not a gospel.

If a phrase doesn't sound like your voice, tweak it. Add, subtract, or swap the language until it feels natural. The goal isn't to memorize lines, it's to protect the *spirit* of the response:
  -Avoiding escalation
  -Avoiding power struggles
  -Avoiding language that harms trust or partnership

Keep the tone student centered and relationship based. The goal is never to "win" a conversation, it's to keep the door open.

Stay grounded when things get heated.

These responses are designed with nervous systems in mind, yours, theirs, and the student's. Parents can bring fear, guilt, or frustration into conversations, and that's human. The language in this book helps you stay steady, calm, and compassionate when tensions start to rise.

Use it before, during, and after conversations.

Before: Review a section before a big meeting or email reply.
During: Keep it nearby for phrases that help you stay calm and on track.
After: Reflect with it when you think, *"That could've gone better."* Adjust, highlight, and make notes for next time.

This book grows with you, and so will your confidence!

Share it. Discuss it. Push back on it.

Use it in staff meetings, parent nights, or teacher training. Write all over the margins. Debate the tone and worth of the responses. Celebrate what lands. Rewrite what doesn't. The goal isn't to agree on every word in this book, it's to raise the quality of every parent conversation in your school.

Keep it close.

On your desk, in your bag, or saved on your phone for those late night parent emails. The more you use it, the more natural the language becomes. Be calm, clear, and human.

Remember:

This book isn't about saying the "perfect" thing. It's about finding the *real* thing to say, the response that protects your professionalism, your peace, and your partnership with parents.

Teaching isn't just what you plan. It's how you communicate!

Let this book help you handle parent conversations with the same care and clarity you give to your students.

I

Blaming/Challenging

Some parents project frustration onto the nearest target, the teacher. These statements may question your competence, fairness, or motives, often said defensively or out of insecurity. The key is to stay grounded and avoid taking the bait. You can model professionalism, defuse ego, and redirect focus back to the student's needs!

"My child doesn't lie/are you calling them a liar?"

You Say:

"I respect your trust in your child and I see honesty is very important to you. My goal isn't to label or accuse anyone but to just share what I observed here. Sometimes a student's perspective doesn't line up with the school's. Let's work together to find a resolution to this so we can keep everything safe and respectful."

* * *

Why It Works:

Affirms the parent's values without questioning them, avoids escalating into a yes/no trap, avoids labeling or accusing the child, and frames the issue as a difference in perspective rather than dishonesty, keeping the focus on collaboration.

"Are you calling me a liar?"

You Say:

"Not at all. I'm not questioning your honesty in any way. I'm only sharing what I observed here at school so we can put our perspectives together to solve this and best support your child."

*　*　*

Why It Works:

Avoids the defensive trap, clarifies the teacher's intent, and frames the conversation as collaboration rather than conflict.

"You just don't understand my child."

You Say:

"I hear that. You know your child in a way no one else can. What I see here at school may look different, and I'd like to learn more from you so I can better support them. Together we can make sure their needs are understood, no matter their environment."

* * *

Why It Works:

Affirms the parent's expertise, lowers defensiveness by honoring their insight, and views the relationship as collaborative rather than oppositional.

"You don't know how to teach."

You Say:

"I'm hearing you're frustrated with how I do things in my class. Teaching your child effectively matters to me, and I want to understand what you feel is missing from my practice. Let's talk through what you're seeing so I can explain my approach and we can find strategies that work for your child."

* * *

Why It Works:

Validates the parent's perspective without arguing or giving in, invites the parent's viewpoint, and shows the moment as a problem solving conversation instead of a personal attack.

"You don't explain things right."

You Say:

"I know different explanations click for different students. I'm always open to trying new ways to make the material clearer. If you've noticed any approaches or strategies that work well for your child in other places, I'd be glad to build on that in my class."

* * *

Why It Works:

Acknowledges the criticism without defensiveness, sees teaching as flexible, and invites parent insight to strengthen the child's learning.

"Why didn't you call me sooner?"

You Say:

"I understand that feels frustrating. My goal is to always keep you informed and to reach out when I have a clear picture of what's going on. Now that we've connected, let's focus on what your child needs now moving forward."

* * *

Why It Works:

Sees the parent's frustration, avoids blame, and shifts the energy from the past missteps to constructive next steps.

"You're a horrible teacher."

You Say:

"I hear your frustration and I'm open to hearing what feels like it isn't working. If we can look at specifics together, I can adjust and make sure your child feels supported."

* * *

Why It Works:

Avoids escalating conflict, validates the parent's emotion, and redirects the insult into a constructive conversation about solutions for the child.

"You embarrassed my child."

You Say:

"Thank you for telling me. The last thing I want is for your child to feel embarrassed in my class. Sometimes I need to redirect behaviors, but I want to do it in a way that protects your child's dignity. I'll reflect on how I handled it and make sure they feel safe and respected moving forward."

* * *

Why It Works:

Acknowledges the harm without defensiveness, protects the child's dignity, and models accountability while committing to repair.

"My child says you shout."

You Say:

"Thanks for bringing that up, I never want students to feel like I'm shouting at them. I may raise my voice at times to get the attention of the whole group, but I work hard to always keep it respectful in tone. If your child felt uncomfortable, I want to know so I can be mindful and make sure they feel comfortable in my class."

* * *

Why It Works:

Recognizes the child's experience without denying it, clarifies intent, and shows willingness to self-reflect which lowers defensiveness and reassures the parent that their child's feelings matter.

"You play favorites."

You Say:

"I hear that concern, and I never want students to feel unequal. My goal is to make sure every child feels they are treated fairly. If your child is feeling overlooked or less than, I want to know so I can be intentional about including them."

* * *

Why It Works:

Acknowledges the perception without arguing, reinforces fairness as a priority, and shifts the focus toward ensuring the child feels seen.

"The test had things you didn't teach."

You Say:

"I'm sorry if there's any confusion on what's been taught vs. what's been tested. Tests in my class reflect what students have had the chance to learn. Let's go through this test together so I can show what was covered in class and where there may have been gaps. That way we can focus on how to support your child moving forward."

* * *

Why It Works:

Validates the frustration without affirming or defensiveness, offers transparency, and shifts the focus from accusation to constructive problem solving.

"You don't care about my child."

You Say:

"I want to be clear, I care about your child's success and safety, even if it doesn't always come across that way. I'm committed to supporting them here at school. If you'd like, we can set up periodic check ins so we can work through your concerns together."

* * *

Why It Works:

Affirms care without backing down, sets a professional boundary against hostility, and redirects the conflict into a structured, mediated space where it can be resolved.

"Other parents warned me about you."

You Say:

"I understand that hearing something like that would make you concerned. My focus is on building trust with you directly and immediately by supporting your child here and now. I'd like to keep our communication open so you can see for yourself how I work with your child."

* * *

Why It Works:

Acknowledges the parent's worry without escalating, avoids arguing about gossip, and redirects the focus toward building trust directly through present actions.

"They aren't learning anything in your class."

You Say:

"I hear how concerning that feels. I want your child to make real progress, so let's look at what they've been working on and where the gaps still are. From there, we can plan supports that will help them show more growth."

* * *

Why It Works:

Sees the frustration without arguing, shifts from a broad accusation to concrete evidence, and invites collaboration on next steps to support learning.

"You're the reason my child won't graduate."

You Say:

"I get how serious this feels because graduation is such an important milestone. My role is to help get your child toward that goal, not become an obstacle in the way. Let's look closely at what's standing in the way right now and make a plan together to help them get to and across that finish line. We can do this."

* * *

Why It Works:

Acknowledges the parent's fear without escalating, reaffirms commitment to the child's success, and shifts the conversation from blame to problem solving and partnership.

"Your class is a joke."

You Say:

"I take teaching seriously, and my goal is always to challenge and support students. Let's look at what feels lacking for your child and how I can make the learning more meaningful for them."

*   *   *

Why It Works:

Defuses a harsh remark without defensiveness, affirms professionalism, and shifts the focus from insult to constructive solutions for the student's growth.

"Maybe this isn't the right career for you."

You Say:

"I'm not going to be defensive, rather, I'd like to know why you say this. Teaching isn't always perfect, but I'm committed to supporting your child and every student in my care. I'd love to discuss your perspective on how your child is learning in my class to see how we can go from there."

* * *

Why It Works:

Disarms a personal attack without defensiveness, centers the conversation on the child's needs, and models professionalism even in the face of hostility.

"You're picking on my child."

You Say:

"The last thing I want is for your child to feel targeted in my class. My role is to hold all students to the same expectations while supporting their success. Let's talk through what your child is experiencing and look at how I can make sure they always feel treated fairly."

* * *

Why It Works:

Acknowledges the seriousness of the accusation without defensiveness, looks at expectations as consistent, and shifts the focus toward understanding and repairing the child's experience.

"You treat her like she's stupid."

You Say:
"I'm so sorry it feels that way, that is never my intention. Your child is capable, and I want her to feel respected and challenged here. I will reflect on how I provide feedback and make sure your child understands clearly that I see her strengths."

* * *

Why It Works:
Acknowledges the harm without defensiveness, reaffirms the child's dignity and capability, and commits to self reflection and repair so the parent feels heard and the child feels valued.

"You're too strict."

You Say:

"I do hold clear boundaries, but my goal is always to create structure where students feel safe to be themselves and able to learn. If something ever feels too rigid for your child, I'm open to hear more so we can find the right balance."

* * *

Why It Works:

Hears the concern without backing down, shows "strict" as structure for safety and learning, and invites collaboration to meet the child's needs.

"You need to be more strict."

You Say:

"I agree that structure and accountability are important. I work to set clear expectations and consistent consequences, while also making sure students feel respected and encouraged. If there are specific strategies that work well at home, I'd be glad to incorporate those here."

* * *

Why It Works:

Partners with the parent's values on discipline, clarifies that structure is already present in the classroom, and frames "strictness" as consistency plus respect, while inviting partnership rather than conflict.

"You're being too hard on them."

You Say:

"I hear your concern. My goal is never to be harsh, but to help them succeed. At school, I set clear limits while also making sure they feel supported. Let's talk through what feels fair so we're on the same page for their growth."

* * *

Why It Works:

Reflects the parent's worry, explains intent calmly, and moves toward shared understanding.

"You're not being hard enough on them."

You Say:

"I understand that concern. In school, I focus on holding students accountable in ways that keep their dignity intact. I've found this approach helps them learn from mistakes without shutting down. Let's look at what's working and where we can adjust together."

* * *

Why It Works:

Validates the concern, explains the supportive accountability approach, and invites collaboration.

"My child doesn't have to respect you."

You Say:

"I am trying to understand your point of view. In class, I focus on modeling respect so students learn how to build positive relationships. Your child doesn't have to agree with me, but they do need to practice respectful interactions for success at school and beyond. I want to work with you to help them develop that skill."

* * *

Why It Works:

Acknowledges the parent without reacting defensively, looks at respect as a life skill rather than obedience, and positions the teacher as a partner in the child's growth.

"That's not how her last teacher did it."

You Say:

"I hear you, transitions can feel more marked when students see teaching styles change. My approach may not be the same as her last teacher, but the goal is always your child's success. If something worked especially well before, I am more than happy to learn about it and see how we can apply it here!"

* * *

Why It Works:

Hears the comparison without any defensiveness, validates the parent's perspective, and shifts the conversation toward blending effective strategies for the child's benefit instead of dismissing other teachers' practices.

"You bully my child."

You Say:

"I hear your concern, and I want to be clear, my role is to make sure your child feels safe and supported here. I'd like to understand what your child has shared with you and then walk through what I've observed. From there, we can talk about what steps will help rebuild the trust your child has for me."

* * *

Why It Works:

Recognizes a serious accusation without defensiveness, centers the child's safety, and shifts the focus toward clarity, respect, and repair instead of conflict.

"You make them cry."

You Say:

"I know that is upsetting to hear. My intent is never to make your child feel hurt, but sometimes strong emotions come up when school feels hard. I want to understand what your child is experiencing and work with you so I can adjust my approach so they feel supported while still learning."

* * *

Why It Works:

Validates the parent's concern, deescalates by clarifying intent, and redirects the focus toward understanding the child's experience and building support.

"They don't want to go to your class."

You Say:

"I hear you. When a student avoids a class, it usually means they're feeling discouraged either by the subject, the teacher, the work, or a mixture of these things. I want to understand what parts feel hard for your child and work together on ways to help them feel more successful here."

* * *

Why It Works:

Keeps the teacher out of a defensive stance, frames avoidance as a signal not defiance, and shifts the focus to partnership in re-engaging the student.

"You treat my child differently due to race."

You Say:

"I take that concern very seriously. Every student deserves to feel respected and included in my classroom. I want to understand what your child has experienced so I can reflect honestly on my own practices. Together we can talk through what will help your child feel seen and safe here."

* * *

Why It Works:

Acknowledges the gravity of the accusation without defensiveness, affirms the student's right to dignity, and shifts the conversation toward listening, reflection, and repair.

"You don't like my child."

You Say:

"I'm sorry it feels that way. Your child matters to me. Sometimes the relationship can get strained when I'm holding them to expectations, but that's because I believe in what they can do. I want to make sure your child feels valued here, so I'm open to hearing what helps."

* * *

Why It Works:

Validates the parent's perception without confirming or denying, separates behavior management from personal feelings, and actively invites partnership to rebuild trust and belonging.

"Why didn't they get an award too?"

You Say:

"I get why that feels disappointing. Awards recognize certain moments, but they don't capture every strength a child brings. I would love to share what I see your child doing well and how we can help them keep shining."

* * *

Why It Works:

Acknowledges the parent's disappointment, exhibits awards as limited, and redirects attention to the child's unique strengths and growth.

"If a student fails, it's the teacher's fault."

You Say:

"I understand why it can feel that way because no one wants to see their child struggle. My role is to provide clear instruction and support, and a student's grade reflects how they are showing understanding. Do you want to look at what's been difficult and what steps we can take together to help them succeed?"

* * *

Why It Works:

Sees the parent's frustration without blame, clarifies the teacher's responsibility, gives an entry to next supportive steps, and shifts the focus from fault to partnership and solutions.

"She only has trouble in your class."

You Say:

"Thank you for sharing that. It helps me know this challenge may feel specific here. I'd like to learn what works well for her in other classes so we can bring some of those strategies into mine and make her feel more successful."

* * *

Why It Works:

Acknowledges the parent's concern without defensiveness, shows the issue as an opportunity to learn from what is working, and invites collaboration to support the child.

"You don't have kids, so you don't know."

You Say:

"I respect that being a parent gives you a perspective I don't have. My role is different though, which is to support your child's learning and welfare at school. Let's combine your insight at home with what I see here so your child gets the best from both of us!"

* * *

Why It Works:

Validates the parent's perspective without minimizing it, sees the teacher's role as complementary rather than competing, and shifts the focus back to teamwork for the child.

"Other teachers don't say that."

You Say:

"I hear you, different teachers may notice different things. What I share comes from what I see in my class, and my goal is to use that information to support your child. If there's something another teacher has found helpful, I'd be glad to learn from that too!"

* * *

Why It Works:

Hears the parent's point, validates that teachers have different perspectives, and shifts the focus toward using all inputs available to strengthen support for the child.

"You're too old to teach this generation."

You Say:

"There's some friction here. Every generation learns differently, and I make it a priority to keep my practice current and connected to today's kids. What matters most is making sure *your* child feels engaged and supported, so that's where I focus my energy."

* * *

Why It Works:

Reflects on the critique without defensiveness, frames age as experience plus adaptability, and brings the focus back to the student's engagement and growth.

"You're too young to teach."

You Say:

"I hear you're concerned about my ability to reach young people if I am young myself. I want to stress that I am in this position because I have earned the proper credentials and gone through the appropriate channels to be where I am today, despite my age. As I gain years of experience, I look forward to improving my practice as a professional, but I assure you I feel ready to lead now."

* * *

Why it works:

Grounds and reflects the parents perspective, explains the "backup" behind the position, models a desire to develop professionally, and maintains teacher's role as a leader of the school.

"You're not good with boys/girls."

You Say:

"I hear you're feeling a difference in how I teach and reach certain kids. My priority is making sure all students receive fair and equal treatment and support. If there are things you've noticed that could help your child feel more seen, heard, or understood, I'd like to learn so I can better connect and make all students feel included at all times."

* * *

Why It Works:

Acknowledges the criticism without shame, opposition, or blame, reaffirms commitment to equity, and shifts the conversation toward specific learning moments and strategies rather than broad judgments.

"Don't tell me how to parent my child."

You Say:

"I'm hearing you, and you know your child best at home. My role is to share what I see at school and how it affects their learning and development. If we put our perspectives together, we can find strategies that work in both environments."

* * *

Why It Works:

Acknowledges the parent's authority, avoids defensiveness, and shows the teacher's role as complementing, not competing with, the parent, keeping the focus on the child's success.

"You should give them the materials."

You Say:

"I appreciate that suggestion, having all materials can make a big difference. I do provide what's needed for class, and when I ask students to bring or find something, it's usually to foster independence. I'll make sure directions stay clear so it always feels manageable."

* * *

Why It Works:

Recognizes the parent's logic, explains the reasoning behind the teacher's practice without defensiveness, and commits to clarity, turning potential criticism into partnership.

"She doesn't need this class."

You Say:

"I understand you want her time to be spent on what feels useful. This class provides skills that connect to every subject, and I want to make sure she's challenged at the right level. If you'd like, we can take a new look at how this class fits into her goals and make sure it stays meaningful for her."

* * *

Why It Works:

Validates the parent's perspective, explains the class's relevance without defensiveness, and frames the conversation around alignment with the child's growth and goals.

II

Behavior and Discipline

When parents defend or excuse their child's behavior, it usually comes from guilt or vulnerability, not hostility. Getting to a place that isn't defensive and that uses evidence helps you hold the line without escalating tension. Clear communication about expectations and consistency across home and school builds trust and accountability!

"They don't do that at home."

You Say:

"I believe you. Kids often show different behaviors in different places. At school, new pressure can bring things out that you may not see at home. Let's look at what's happening here at school and think together about how to help your child feel steady in both places."

* * *

Why It Works:

Grounds the parent's perspective without being defensive about truthfulness, explains without blame, and opens the door to collaboration.

"They do the same thing at home."

You Say:

"It sounds like we're both seeing the same challenges. That means the behavior is consistent, and we can work together on strategies that carry over from school to home. The more your child receives the same message in both environments, the stronger their progress will be!"

* * *

Why It Works:

Validates the parent's observation, looks at consistency as useful data, and emphasizes shared strategies rather than blame.

"Did they behave today?"

You Say:

"I would love to tell you how the day went! Remember, I focus on how your child is learning and interacting, not just if they were well-behaved. Today I noticed ___, and this is what we're working on to help them keep growing."

* * *

Why It Works:

Shifts the conversation away from labeling behavior, views it in terms of learning and growth, and gives the parent something concrete without fueling shame.

"Does she listen?"

You Say:

"She does listen, and like with all students, sometimes it may takes reminders or redirections. What I have really noticed is that when she feels clear on the routines and expectations, she's able to focus and follow through."

* * *

Why It Works:

Avoids a simple yes/no that could feel judgmental, views listening as a skill that grows with support, and keeps the focus on positive strategies instead of just labeling the child's behavior.

"You can yell at him if you want to."

You Say:

"I appreciate you trusting me, but I don't use yelling as a strategy. My approach is to keep expectations firm and consistent while making sure your child always feels respected. That way, discipline helps students learn rather than shut down."

* * *

Why It Works:

Acknowledges the parent's frustration, sets a firm boundary against harmful discipline, and shows the teacher's approach as respectful yet effective.

"You have my permission to hit him."

You Say:

"No, I can't do that. I won't use physical discipline, my job is to keep every child *safe*. If you're feeling upset about his behavior, let's find safe, effective ways to address it."

* * *

Why It Works:

Sets an immediate safety boundary, refuses harm without shaming the parent, redirects the energy into formal, constructive supports so the child is protected and the family's concerns are addressed.

"He said he's the only one who gets in trouble."

You Say:

"Thank you for bringing this to my attention. Kids often notice their own consequences more than what their peers are experiencing. I can assure you that expectations, consequences, and follow through in my class are consistent for everyone. I will work to make sure he understands that so he feels treated fairly."

* * *

Why It Works:

Acknowledges the child's perception without dismissing it, takes another look at fairness, and reassures the parent that consistency is maintained for all students.

"We teach them it's OK to hit back."

You Say:

"I know you want your child to feel strong and able to protect themselves. At school, my role is to keep every student safe, and that's why we teach other ways to handle conflict. I'd like to partner with you on strategies that give your child the same confidence without putting them at any risk."

* * *

Why It Works:

Validates the parent's intent, sets a clear safety boundary, and frames self-protection around nonviolent strategies that preserve dignity and reduce harm.

"He's bad."

You Say:

"I hear your frustration, but I don't see your child as 'bad.' What I see are behaviors that might make school harder for him. Together we can focus on what's driving those behaviors and how to build on his strengths."

* * *

Why It Works:

Interrupts harmful labeling without shaming the parent, sees behavior as separate from identity, and points toward strengths and solutions.

"Why are you always writing them up?"

You Say:

"I never want write ups to feel like punishment since they're meant to document patterns and give us a chance to intervene at the right time. Let's look at what's leading up to these situations and find ways to help your child without needing referrals."

* * *

Why It Works:

Sees the parent's frustration, observes write-ups as part of a support process, and shifts the focus from blame to root causes and proactive strategies.

"She only cares about boys."

You Say:

"This is something we see often. This age brings strong social interests, and that can sometimes distract from learning. What I want is to first help her feel valued for her strengths, then keep her focused on goals that build her confidence beyond relationships. Do we want to start talking about some of those goals with her now?"

* * *

Why It Works:

Acknowledges the parent's frustration without shaming the student, frames the behavior as a developmental stage, and shifts focus toward identity, strengths, and long term growth.

"Don't let him use any screens."

You Say:

"I understand you want to limit screen time for your child. At school, some lessons and tools do require technology. What I can do is let you know when screens are being used and focus his time on the learning goals, not just the device."

* * *

Why It Works:

Respects the parent's boundary, explains the reality of classroom practice, and offers transparency and balance instead of outright refusal or compliance.

"I'm going to send him away."

You Say:

"That sounds heavy, and I can hear how much stress you're under. Big changes like being sent 'away' to another place can deeply affect a child. My goal is to make sure he feels supported at school, no matter what is happening at home. If you're OK with it, I can connect you with resources that might help before making a big step like this."

* * *

Why It Works:

Understands the parent's stress without judgment, centers the child's well being, and redirects toward supportive resources instead of reacting with shock or criticism.

III

Academic Pressure and Grade Concerns

Grades and data can be emotional currency for parents. When they panic about numbers, it's not about you, it's about their own fear of failure, judgment, or lost opportunities. Responding calmly, emphasizing growth and evidence, and explaining your grading philosophy can shift the conversation from blame to collaboration.

"Why did my child get this grade?"

You Say:

"I hear your question. This grade reflects how your child has been showing their understanding on assignments and assessments. I want to walk you through what I've seen in class and then talk about what supports can help them grow."

* * *

Why It Works:

Affirms the question, explains the grade objectively and with evidence, and pivots to next steps for supports for improvement.

"You're giving too much homework."

You Say:

"I hear that it feels like a lot of schoolwork at home. My intention with homework is to reinforce skills, not to overwhelm. Let's look at what's manageable for your child and adjust so it supports their learning without adding stress."

* * *

Why It Works:

Reflects the parent's concern, explains purpose and intention behind homework, and invites problem solving together as a team.

"You're not giving enough homework."

You Say:

"I understand that you want to see more practice at home. I focus on making sure your student can use class time for the heavy lifting. Homework for my class reinforces key skills without burning students out. If you'd like, I can share extra practice ideas for home to support your child."

* * *

Why It Works:

Acknowledges the concern without deflecting, explains approach in a relatable way that centers the student's well being, and offers proactive next steps for support.

"He didn't have time to study."

You Say:

"I understand, life outside school can get really busy. What matters is finding ways for him to keep learning, even in small chunks. I can share strategies or ways to do extra practice that fit into short periods of time so he still feels prepared and part of the learning."

* * *

Why It Works:

Recognizes the parent's reality without judgment, shifts the focus from blame to problem-solving, and offers concrete supports that reduce pressure while keeping learning on track.

"He doesn't tell me what he needs to get."

You Say:

"I understand, that's common for students and frustrating for parents. I'll always make sure assignments and expectations are clear in class, and I can share a way for you to see them directly too. That way you don't have to rely only on him remembering to explain."

* * *

Why It Works:

Acknowledges the parent's frustration without blame, frames it as a developmental challenge, and offers a practical system that builds trust and reduces miscommunication without harping on bad habits.

"We don't believe in grades."

You Say:

"I can respect that. Grades don't capture everything a child can do. At school, I'm required to report grades, but what really matters most to me is the learning behind them. I can always share specific strengths and areas for growth so you see more than just a number or letter."

* * *

Why It Works:

Affirms the parent's belief, sets a boundary around grading requirements, and gears the conversation toward meaningful learning and progress.

"Can you offer tutoring?"

You Say:

"Wanting extra support shows how much you care about your child's success. While I can't provide tutoring myself all the time, I can always share resources, strategies, and programs that give your child any extra practice they need. Let's make sure the support feels like something you or your family can do with your child."

* * *

Why It Works:

Hears the parent's concern, sets realistic limits without shutting them down, and redirects toward concrete solutions that keep the child's growth central.

"Will you tutor her more?"

You Say:

"I can see how much you want her to have extra support. I may not be able to provide private tutoring myself, but I can certainly give her extra help during school time. I can also always share resources or referrals for additional tutoring if you'd like. That way she's getting what she needs."

* * *

Why It Works:

Acknowledges the parent's request with empathy, sets a clear boundary around the teacher's role, and redirects toward realistic supports so the child doesn't go without help.

"Your grading isn't fair."

You Say:

"I don't want to come across as unfair. My goal is always to grade in a way that shows what your child has learned, never to discourage them. Let's go through assignments from class together so you can see how we arrived at the grade and we can talk about next steps for improvement."

* * *

Why It Works:

Listens to the parent's frustration without defensiveness, emphasizes fairness and purpose, and shifts the conversation toward transparency and solutions.

"I did it for them."

You Say:

"I appreciate how much you want to help your child. The challenge is that when the work isn't their own, I can't see what they really understand. What helps most is if I see their thinking, even with mistakes that way I know how to support them better, which is really what's best for your child."

* * *

Why It Works:

Affirms the parent's care, explains the downside of doing the work without shaming, and views mistakes as valuable information for growth.

"Why is he still behind?"

You Say:

"I know it's discouraging to feel that your child is behind. Progress can take time, especially when a skill is tough to build. I can show you where he's grown and where we still need to focus, and then together we'll make a plan to help him keep moving forward."

* * *

Why It Works:

Acknowledges the parent's frustration, frames the situation as progress-in-process, and offers transparency plus partnership to replace blame with action.

"He's too smart/He's just failing because he's bored."

You Say:

"I can see why you feel that way, bright students sometimes do check out when they don't feel challenged enough. Let's first look at where he is excelling and where any gaps are showing up. Then we can match the work to his level and keep him engaged while still holding him accountable."

* * *

Why It Works:

Validates the parent's view of their child's intelligence, examines failure as a mix of engagement and skill gaps, and shifts the focus toward tailored support and accountability.

"She just needs one-on-one attention."

You Say:

"I know individual attention can make a big difference. In class, I work to balance that with the needs of all my students. What I can definitely do is give her focused support during certain times and share strategies you can always use at home to keep building her confidence."

* * *

Why It Works:

Recognizes the parent's belief, explains classroom realities without defensiveness, and offers both targeted support and practical partnership to meet the child's needs.

"She's like me, I'm bad at math."

You Say:

"I hear you, a lot of parents feel that way about different subjects. What I want your child to see is that struggling at something doesn't mean she's 'bad' at it. With steady practice and support, she can build confidence and see herself as capable."

* * *

Why It Works:

Appreciates and relates the parent's honesty, interrupts negative self talk, and frames math struggles as a skill building process rather than a fixed identity.

"Can they have more time to finish?"

You Say:

"I understand wanting your child to have all the time they need. In class, I can provide extensions or adjust deadlines when it supports their learning. Let's figure out together what extra time looks like so it builds up their confidence without letting the work become too much."

* * *

Why It Works:

Shows flexibility, balances empathy with structure, and keeps the focus on growth rather than punishment.

"Can you give them extra credit?"

You Say:

"I get why you are asking that. Extra credit can help, but it works best when it builds on what your child is already learning. Instead of just adding points, I'm glad to offer meaningful options that reinforce skills. This way the extra credit really supports their progress."

* * *

Why It Works:

Validates the parent's request, frames extra credit as purposeful learning, and protects fairness while still offering a path forward.

"Can you do/write it for them?"

You Say:

"I get why you would want to relieve some of that pressure for your child. My goal is for them to practice expressing their own thinking, especially when it isn't perfect. What I can do to support is give them sentence starters and extra scaffolds so they feel like they can do it themselves."

* * *

Why It Works:

Shows understanding of the parent's instinct to help, explains the importance of student ownership, and offers a supportive alternative that protects independence without dismissing the parent.

"He just needs to pass."

You Say:

"I get that, you're focused on making sure he moves forward and advances. I want that too, and I want him to really understand the material. *Passing* means he's ready for what comes next. Let's figure out the quickest, most supportive way to help him earn it."

* * *

Why It Works:

Acknowledges the parent's urgency without judgment, frames "passing" as meaningful mastery, and invites collaboration toward a solution that supports both progress and learning.

"She doesn't want to go to college."

You Say:

"I hear that, college isn't the only path to success! What matters is helping her find direction and purpose. I'll keep focusing on the skills and confidence she'll need for whatever future she chooses."

* * *

Why It Works:

Affirms the parent's honesty, removes stigma around non college paths, and puts the goal as preparing the student for a meaningful and capable future, not one single route.

"I don't allow failing grades."

You Say:

"I understand, nobody wants to see their child struggle. I'm not out to let students fail but to help them *earn* success through support and accountability. I'll keep offering chances to improve, but their grade has to reflect what your child has shown they can do."

* * *

Why It Works:

Acknowledges the parent's protective instinct, reinforces fairness and academic integrity, and posits "failing" as part of a growth process supported by clear expectations.

"Can't you just pass him?"

You Say:

"I understand why you would want that. No parent wants to see their child struggle. But passing without the skills won't set him up for success. What I can do is show you exactly where he's behind and what supports we can put in place so he can truly earn the grade."

* * *

Why It Works:

Validates the parent's desire to see their child succeed, sets a professional boundary against grade inflation, and frames the focus on real learning and long term success.

"I don't want them to go to college."

You Say:

"I hear you, college isn't the right path for everyone. What I want is to make sure your child leaves school with the skills and confidence to choose from many options, whether that's a trade, career, or higher education. Let's focus on keeping those doors open so the choice is truly theirs."

* * *

Why It Works:

Affirms the parent's perspective, avoids pushing a single track, and looks at school as preparation for choice and opportunity rather than a forced path.

"He'll lose his scholarship if he fails your class."

You Say:

"I know how much that scholarship means. My objective isn't to see it taken away but to make sure he really has the skills to succeed in and beyond this class. Let's see where to put supports in place so he has the best chance to earn his grade here and keep the scholarship."

* * *

Why It Works:

Sees the high stakes, reassures the parent that the teacher is not the adversary, and shifts the focus from pressure on the grade to concrete steps that strengthen the student's performance.

"I dropped out of school and I'm fine."

You Say:

"I get that you've made your own path, and I really respect that. For your child, finishing school will opens as many doors as possible, whether they choose college, a trade, or something else. My goal is always to help them feel capable so they can decide their future with more options."

* * *

Why It Works:

Honors the parent's lived experience, avoids judgment, and views school completion as expanding choices rather than following a single track.

"He won't be doing summer school."

You Say:

"I understand summer school can feel like a big request or requirement. If that's absolutely not an option, then we will need to look at other ways to make sure he gets caught up. I want to work with you on a plan that keeps him on track without falling further behind."

* * *

Why It Works:

Respects the parent's stance without arguing, sets an expectation that progress still requires support, and shifts the focus toward alternatives that prioritize the child's success.

IV

Mental, Medical, & Emotional Concerns

These statements often come from fear and exhaustion, from parent or child. Parents facing a child's anxiety, depression, or burnout want reassurance that someone else sees their struggle. Your tone and words can become part of the student's support system. Compassion first, solutions second!

"She has anxiety."

You Say:

"Anxiety can make school feel overwhelming. I'll look for signs here and create space where she feels safe and steady. Together, we can share strategies so she knows we have her back."

* * *

Why It Works:

Validates the parent, normalizes anxiety as something manageable, and emphasizes consistent support across environments to reduce stress for the child.

"He is depressed."

You Say:

"That must be heavy for both of you. At school I'll make sure he has space to feel safe and supported. Can you share what helps him most at home so we can keep things consistent?"

* * *

Why It Works:

Feels the weight, centers care, and uses a reflective question to invite the parent's expertise instead of repeating the same teacher-centered script.

"He was up all night playing video games."

You Say:

"I see, thanks for letting me know. That definitely impacts his focus at school. While I will always support him here, the biggest difference will come from healthy routines at home. If you're open to it, I can share strategies other families use to balance screen time so students feel rested and ready to learn."

* * *

Why It Works:

Acknowledges the parent's concern without judgment, connects the issue to learning in a clear way, and shifts the focus toward consistency and healthy routines. Offers solutions that keep the teacher in a supportive role rather than a critical one.

"She just doesn't care."

You Say:

"I can see why it feels that way, it's certainly hard to watch your child pull back. Usually when students seem not to care, it's a sign of frustration or disconnection, not plain apathy. I'll work on finding what motivates her again and keep you updated on what seems to help."

* * *

Why It Works:

Sees the parent's discouragement, presents the behavior as a signal rather than a flaw, and restores hope by focusing on engagement instead of blame.

"He doesn't want to wake up in the morning."

You Say:

"That is a lot for both of you. Sometimes these types of morning struggles can signal stress, sleep issues, or feeling something deeper. I will keep things steady here, and we can work together on routines or supports that make mornings easier for him. If you're both open to it, we can also get him connected to a counselor."

* * *

Why It Works:

Understands the parent's frustration without blame, frames the behavior as a signal rather than laziness, and offers partnership and professional, practical support to improve the child's readiness for school.

"They don't want to come to school."

You Say:

"I hear that, and it's tough when a child resists school. Kids sometimes avoid school when they feel discouraged, anxious, or disconnected. Let's talk about what might be driving that for your child, and how we can make school feel like a place they want to be."

* * *

Why It Works:

Recognizes the struggle without judgment, shows school avoidance as a signal not defiance, and invites collaboration to rebuild connection.

"She doesn't care about friends at all."

You Say:

"Thank you for sharing that, we know every child is different in how they connect socially. I will pay attention to how she interacts here and make sure she still feels included, even if she prefers being on her own. Together we can support her confidence so she feels comfortable in both her learning *and* her relationships with her peers."

* * *

Why It Works:

Validates the parent's observation, normalizes differences in social development, and directs the focus toward belonging and confidence rather than to a problem.

"She's not eating right."

You Say:

"Thanks for sharing that with me, we know nutrition affects how a child feels and learns each day. At school, I'll keep an eye on her appetite and energy, and I can let you know what I notice. Together we can support her so she feels healthy and steady here."

* * *

Why It Works:

Hears the parent's concern, connects eating habits to learning in a nonjudgmental way, and offers observation plus partnership to help the child feel supported.

"I think he needs medicine."

You Say:

"I hear your concern about their behavior patterns or focus. As a teacher, I cannot recommend or prescribe medication, but I can share what I've observed in class. If you like, I will document what I see and communicate with you/your child's healthcare provider so you can have a clearer picture before making any decisions."

* * *

Why It Works:

Respects the parent's worry, sets a clear professional boundary, and offers constructive support that keeps the focus on informed decision-making for the child.

V

Family, Home, or Custody Issues

Behind many classroom struggles is chaos at home. Parents might overshare, deflect, or break down entirely. You're not their therapist, but you can be their anchor. Acknowledging hardships without judgment helps preserve student dignity while connecting families to appropriate school supports.

"I just lost my job."

You Say:

"I'm really sorry to hear that. I can only imagine how tough it might feel right now. Please know your child's support at school will not change. If there are resources or adjustments that might ease things for your family right now, I'll do what I can to connect you."

* * *

Why It Works:

Centers empathy first, reassures stability for the child, and offers practical help without prying, reducing shame and building trust.

"We are in a custody battle."

You Say:

"Thank you for letting me know, I understand how stressful that can be for a family. My only role is to make sure your child feels safe, cared for, and focused on learning here. Please keep me updated on anything I should be aware of that may affect the support your child needs through this time."

* * *

Why It Works:

Acknowledges the parent's stress without taking sides, sets a clear boundary around the teacher's role, and emphasizes stability and consistency for the child.

"Will you come to our house?"

You Say (to accept):

"If it helps your child, I'd be happy to come! Let's set up the proper arrangements through the office. That way everything is safe, professional, and focused on supporting their learning."

You Say (to say "No"):

"I really appreciate the offer. To keep things professional, I don't meet students at their homes. What I can always do is set up a time to meet at school or share resources that support learning at home."

* * *

Why It Works (Yes):

Affirms the parent's request, sets conditions around boundaries and professionalism, and frames the visit as structured, school-sponsored support.

Why It Works (No):

Thanks the parent and acknowledges the request without shaming or hurting feelings, sets a clear boundary, and redirects toward appropriate alternatives.

"We're losing our home."

You Say:

"I'm so sorry you're going through that. That's a heavy stress for any family. At school, I will make sure your child feels stable and supported, even while things are uncertain at home. I can also connect you with resources that may help ease the transition."

* * *

Why It Works:

Shares the gravity of the loss with empathy, reassures consistency for the child, and offers practical support without judgment.

"We are moving but we haven't told them."

You Say:

"I appreciate the heads up. I'll keep that private until you share it with your child. Moves can bring big emotions, so when the time comes, I'll be here to support them at school and help keep routines steady."

* * *

Why It Works:

Respects the parent's timing, reassures confidentiality, and anticipates the child's emotional needs so the transition feels safe and supported.

"We will be gone for a month."

You Say:

"Thanks for letting me know, we can start now on a plan to keep things as steady as possible for when your child returns. A month away is a big gap, so we have to help your child stay connected to learning during that time. I'll prepare what I can and we can talk about realistic ways to keep them on track while you're away."

* * *

Why It Works:

Recognizes the family's plan without judgment, sets a boundary around the impact of lost time, and offers proactive support to reduce learning loss.

"We had a big loss in the family."

You Say:

"I'm very sorry to hear that. Grief can affect kids in ways that don't always show up right away. I'll keep an eye on how your child is doing and make space for them here if they need it. Please let me know if there's anything specific that would comfort or support them during the school day."

* * *

Why It Works:

Meets the parent with empathy, normalizes grief's impact on children, and reassures that the child's needs will be noticed and supported at school.

"We are going to transfer them to a better school."

You Say:

"I hear you. You want the best for your child. If you've already decided to transfer, I'll make sure the move is smooth and everything on my end is ready. If this is a concern you'd like me to address so your child can stay, tell me what would help and I'll do my part to fix it."

* * *

Why It Works:

Validates the parent's intent, avoids a power struggle, keeps the child's needs central, and offers either practical next steps (transition) or a concrete path to resolve the concern.

"We are thinking of homeschooling."

You Say:

"You want what feels right for your child. Homeschooling can be a big decision, and my goal is the same as yours: your child's success. I can share what I've seen academically and socially so you have a full picture before deciding their next step."

* * *

Why It Works:

Respects the parent's autonomy, keeps the tone open and not defensive, and positions the teacher as a supportive professional offering insight rather than persuasion.

"You don't know what goes on at home."

You Say:

"You're right, I don't see everything your child experiences at home. That's why your perspective is so important to me. If you're open to sharing, I'd like to learn what's hard at home so I can better support your child here at school."

* * *

Why It Works:

Affirms the parent's expertise, avoids defensiveness, and examines the comment as an opening for partnership, keeping the child's needs central.

"We can't afford (school activity)."

You Say:

"I hear you, money should never be the reason your child misses out at school. Let me check what options we have, whether it's waivers, fund raising, or other support alternatives, so your child can still feel included."

* * *

Why It Works:

Acknowledges financial stress without shame, reassures inclusion, and points toward practical solutions that protect the child's sense of belonging.

"Don't tell her father/mother." (If legal guardian)

You Say:

"I hear your request, and I want to be clear that I can't withhold information from a legal guardian. My role is to stay neutral and focus on your child's well-being. If there are custody documents or legal agreements I should be aware of, please share them so I can follow them correctly."

* * *

Why It Works:

Acknowledges the parent's request without agreeing, sets a firm legal boundary, and keeps the focus on protecting the child while following proper procedures.

"Their father/mother is no longer in the picture."

You Say:

"Thank you for sharing that with me. I know changes at home can feel big for a child. Here at school, I'll make sure they feel supported and not singled out. If there's anything specific that would help them feel steady, please let me know. I'm glad to work with you."

* * *

Why It Works:

Pays attention to the family change without prying, communicates stability at school, and invites collaboration so the child feels secure and included.

VI

Religious, Cultural, or Political Issues

These moments require the highest professionalism. Stay factual, respectful, and legally aligned. You're not debating beliefs; you're clarifying boundaries and protecting every student's right to feel safe and included.

"We don't celebrate (holiday)."

You Say:

"Thank you for sharing that with me. I'll make sure your child feels comfortable and respected during holiday activities. We can plan alternatives so they can be included without feeling any pressure to take part in traditions that your family doesn't observe."

* * *

Why It Works:

Validates the parent's beliefs, protects the child from exclusion, and frames the teacher as a partner in honoring family and self identity while maintaining belonging in the group.

"He's not allowed to read/watch that."

You Say:

"Thank you for letting me know, I respect your boundaries at home. At school, I'll make sure to provide alternate options so he's still engaged and learning without going against your wishes."

* * *

Why It Works:

Acknowledges the parent's values without argument, sets a cooperative tone, and reassures them that the child won't be excluded from learning opportunities.

"I don't want him to be gay."

You Say:

"I hear how strongly you feel, and I want to be clear that my role is to make sure every child feels safe, respected, and valued at school. Your child deserves that care no matter what. Here, I will support, protect, and respect all my students so they can learn and grow without fear."

* * *

Why It Works:

Recognizes the parent's intensity without agreeing, sets a clear boundary of safety and dignity, and centers the child's right to protection and respect.

"My child isn't trans."

You Say:

"I know that these conversations can be difficult. My role at school is to make sure your child feels safe and respected for who they are. My only goal is to continue to support them here so they can focus on learning while you work through this as a family."

* * *

Why It Works:

Sees the tension without taking sides, sets a clear boundary of safety and respect for the student, and keeps the teacher's focus on the child's well being in the school environment.

"Please use (their deadname)."

You Say:

"I hear your request. In our classroom, though, we call students by the names they identify with. That's how we ensure every child feels respected and safe here. I know this may feel complicated, but my responsibility is to honor your child's dignity while also following school policies and best practices. We can keep the conversation open, but I will be using the name your child identifies with."

* * *

Why it works:

Hears the parent's request without approving it, explains current best practices* and centers student dignity and respect, while keeping the door open to the parent's growth.

*MAJOR NOTE: This is, unfortunately, not an option for teachers in some states, proceed with care and caution!

"You're indoctrinating my child."

You Say:

"I hear your concern. My role isn't to tell students what to believe, it's to teach skills and knowledge so they can think for themselves. If something ever feels concerning to you, don't hesitate to let me know and I'll be glad to explain the lesson and how it connects to our learning goals."

* * *

Why It Works:

Affirms the parent's fear without agreeing, clarifies the teacher's professional role, and redirects the focus toward transparency and student independence instead of ideology.

"You aren't teaching CRT are you?"

You Say:

"I gather you're concerned about Critical Race Theory. It isn't a part of K-12 curriculum here but what I do teach is respect, history, and critical thinking so students learn how to engage with different perspectives in safe, appropriate ways. If you ever want to check out what we are doing in class as far as lessons and assignments, I would be happy to share."

* * *

Why It Works:

Defuses the loaded question without defensiveness, clarifies curriculum boundaries, and puts the teacher's role as focusing on respect and appropriate learning.

VII

Overstepping and Involvement

Over involved parents often mean well but struggle to let their child develop independence. The trick is to validate their concern while establishing your professional boundaries. Balance warmth with firmness and remind them that responsibility builds confidence.

"Can I be a chaperone?" (To say no)

You Say:

"Thank you for wanting to be involved! I really appreciate that. For this trip, we already have the chaperones set through our school policy, so I can't add more. If you'd like, I can share other ways to help out that still make a big difference for the class."

* * *

Why It Works:

Acknowledges the parent's willingness, sets a clear boundary without blame, and redirects their energy into appropriate opportunities for involvement.

"Can I bring cupcakes?" (To say no)

You Say:

"Thanks for wanting to do something special for the class! That means a lot. Right now, we aren't able to bring in outside food for safety and health reasons. If you'd like, I can suggest another way to celebrate that your child and classmates will still enjoy."

* * *

Why It Works:

Appreciates the parent's intent, sets a clear "no" without guilt, and redirects their generosity toward an acceptable alternative.

"Can I help in your classroom?"

You Say (Yes):

"Absolutely! I'd love to have you involved. It makes a big difference when students see families engaged at school. Let's set up a time and way that works well so your help supports the kids without disrupting their routines."

You Say (No):

"Thank you for offering, I really appreciate your willingness. For now, I need to keep the classroom routine consistent for the students. If you'd like, I can suggest other ways to be involved that still make a difference without being in the classroom itself."

* * *

Why It Works (Yes):

Welcomes the parent, ties their involvement to student benefit, and sets boundaries around structure.

Why It Works (No):

Acknowledges generosity, gently holds the boundary, and redirects to alternatives so the parent doesn't feel shut out.

"Can he switch into your class?"

You Say:

"I appreciate that! It means a lot that you want him in my class. Class placements have to go through administration, but I can share my availability and support with whatever decision they make to ensure he's set up for success!"

* * *

Why It Works:

Accepts the compliment with gratitude, keeps boundaries clear around placement decisions, and shows willingness to collaborate with the system and the family for the child's benefit.

"My child is special."

You Say:

"I agree with you! Every child brings unique strengths to the table. My goal is to notice what makes your child shine and help them grow in ways that build on those gifts."

* * *

Why It Works:

Affirms the parent's pride without exaggeration, sees "special" as a perspective based on strengths, and centers the child's growth in school, not ego.

VIII

Disengaged and Absent Parenting

When parents seem checked out, it's usually burnout, not straight up apathy. They may be overwhelmed, embarrassed, or just simply surviving. Approaching parents with empathy rather than judgment can open countless doors of communication. The goal is never to shame. It's to reengage parents as partners, however small the steps.

"You get paid to teach, not me."

You Say:

"I understand, teaching is my job, and I take it very seriously. What helps most is when home and school work *together*, because kids make the most improvement and progress when they feel that connection to and support in both places."

* * *

Why It Works:

Acknowledges the parent's frustration without defensiveness, reaffirms professional responsibility, and frames the situation as teamwork rather than shifting the burden.

"Don't call me anymore."

You Say:

"I understand your request. My goal in reaching out is always to support your child. If my phone calls feel like too much, we can use another way to stay in touch like email, written notes, or scheduled check ins, so you still know how your child is doing."

* * *

Why It Works:

Validates the parent's boundary, explains the purpose of contact, and offers flexible options that preserve communication without escalating.

"He's not even my kid."

You Say:

"I understand. That can make things complicated. I really appreciate that you're still showing up for him. I'll keep helping him here and make sure communication from the school and I stays simple and clear for you."

* * *

Why It Works:

Acknowledges the emotional distance or frustration behind the statement, expresses appreciation without guilt tripping, and keeps the focus on stability and teamwork for the child's sake.

"I don't need to meet with you."

You Say:

"I respect that, you know your time and priorities best. I'll continue to keep you updated through other channels, and if concerns come up that really require us to talk, I'll reach back out so we can decide together what next steps are necessary."

* * *

Why It Works:

Recognizes the parent's choice, avoids any power struggle, and leaves the door open for future communication while keeping the child's needs at the center.

IX

Praise Toward Teacher

These are the rare breaths of air in the storm. Acknowledge them, but don't get too comfortable. Praise from parents can range from genuine to a setup before a complaint. Either way, accept it graciously and use it to strengthen the relationship and your credibility.

"You're an amazing teacher."

You Say:

"Thank you, that really means a lot. I feel blessed and lucky to work with your child, and seeing their progress is simply the best part of this job."

* * *

Why It Works:

Accepts the compliment sincerely, keeps the focus student-centered, and models humility while still acknowledging the praise.

"You're the best teacher she's ever had."

You Say:

"That's really kind of you to say! She brings so much to this classroom, and it's been a privilege to be a part of her learning and growing. I'm so glad she feels safe and seen here."

* * *

Why It Works:

Accepts the compliment with joy, turns the spotlight back onto the student's strengths, and reinforces the teacher's role as someone who notices and values the child deeply.

"I don't know how you do it."

You Say:

"Thank you, some days are a challenge. But what keeps me going is seeing students grow and having supporting families like yours. It means a lot to know the work is noticed."

* * *

Why It Works:

Receives the compliment with gratitude, humanizes the teaching effort without complaining, and ties the recognition back to the shared goal of student growth.

"He talks about your class all the time."

You Say:

"I love hearing that! It tells me he is connecting with what we are doing. I'll keep building on that excitement so he consistently feels ownership and pride over his learning here."

* * *

Why It Works:

Graciously accepts the positive feedback, ties the enthusiasm back to student engagement, and centers the focus on continued growth.

"You're their favorite teacher."

You Say:

"That means a lot to hear. My hope is for all students to see the best versions of themselves while they're learning with me. I'll keep encouraging them to bring that same grit and confidence into all of their classes."

* * *

Why It Works:

Accepts the compliment with gratitude without making it too personal, reinforces the teacher's professional role, and redirects the focus toward the student's growth and consistency across settings.

X

Threats and Escalations

These moments test your composure the most. Parents may yell, threaten, or attempt intimidation when they feel powerless. Your calm professionalism is your shield and your power statement. Set boundaries, document everything, and never, ever match their volume or tone.

"This isn't over."

You Say:

"I hear you. For now, I'll document our conversation and involve administration so we can address your concerns through the proper channels."

* * *

Why It Works:

Acknowledges the intensity without fueling it, sets a boundary by moving the issue into official channels, and centers the conversation on the student's well-being.

"We will take this to the principal."

You Say:

"I understand. You have every right to do that. My goal is the same as yours, which is to ensure your child's success and well-being. I'll share everything I can openly, and I'm glad to meet with the principal together if that feels helpful."

* * *

Why It Works:

Respects the parent's authority without defensiveness, keeps the focus on shared goals, and frames escalation as an opportunity for transparency and collaboration.

"We will sue/go to the board."

You Say:

"I understand you want to take this seriously, and you have every right to seek legal support. My role is to focus on your child's safety and learning while following school policies. I'll make sure administration is included on this conversation so your concerns are handled properly."

* * *

Why It Works:

Acknowledges the parent's right without escalating, maintains professionalism, and redirects the conflict into official channels rather than a personal battle.

"I pay your salary!"

You Say:

"I hear you are frustrated. I want to be clear, my role is to teach and protect all students, and that doesn't change based on this conversation. I'm committed to your child's success, and I'd like us to stay focused on what helps them learn."

* * *

Why It Works:

Sees the parent's anger without indulging it, reinforces professional boundaries, and pivots firmly back to the child's learning and well-being.

"I"ll see you in the parking lot."

You Say:

"I need to stop here, I can't continue this. I'll get an administrator right now."

* * *

Why It Works:

Ends the exchange immediately, prioritizes teacher safety, and moves the situation into official channels without argument.

XI

Safety and Legal Concerns

Any statement or move that hints at danger, abuse, or illegal activity must trigger your mandated reporter instincts. Your job is not to investigate but to act. Keep empathy at the center, stay factual, and follow legal protocol without hesitation!

"How do I know my child will be safe?"

You Say:

"That's the most important question you could ask. At school we have clear routines and safeguards in place, and I watch closely to make sure your child feels secure. If you ever have a worry, I want you to reach out right away so we can address it together."

* * *

Why It Works:

Centers the parent's concern as valid, offers concrete reassurance without over-promising, and invites an open channel of communication to build trust.

"My child needs their phone on them."

You Say:

"I know, phones can feel like a lifeline, especially for families. In class we have limits so learning isn't disrupted. What I will do is make sure your child knows when and how they have access, and if there's an emergency, you can always reach the school right away."

If they still push back because of safety:

You Say:

"I get it, that fear is real. Safety is our top priority too. We have emergency plans so students are never left unprotected, and phones are part of those in a controlled way. I'll make sure you know how we handle communication during emergencies and if you want, we can talk this over with a member of admin to get a clearer picture."

* * *

Why It Works:

Acknowledges the parent's need for connection, explains boundaries clearly, and offers a safety net so the parent still feels reassured. Avoids minimizing the reality of school violence, and sees safety as a shared goal while reinforcing structured procedures that protect all students.

"She's being bullied."

You Say:

"I'm really sorry to hear that, no child should feel unsafe here. I'll take this seriously and look into what's happening right away. Let's stay in close contact as I address it so your child knows we're working together to keep her safe."

* * *

Why It Works:

Centers the child's safety, validates the parent's concern without hesitation, and commits to immediate action and ongoing communication, building trust and reassurance.

"I have reported bullying, but nothing happens."

You Say:

"I hear how frustrating that feels. Bullying is serious, and no student should feel unsafe. Let's go over what actions have already been taken, and then map out clear next steps so your child feels real support."

* * *

Why It Works:

Validates the parent's frustration, reinforces commitment to safety, and shifts from past inaction to concrete forward motion.

"We saw you drinking/smoking a cigarette."

You Say:

"Thanks for sharing that. What I do outside of school is separate from my role here, but I want to assure you it doesn't affect how I care for or teach my students. My focus at school is always professionalism and your child's safety and education."

* * *

Why It Works:

Acknowledges the parent's observation without defensiveness, sets a boundary between personal and professional life, and calmly redirects the conversation back to the teacher's integrity and the child's learning.

"We saw you (doing something illegal)."

You Say:

"That's a major thing to say. What happens outside of school is a private matter, but I'm committed to staying professional and focused on your child's learning. If you believe something needs to be addressed, I encourage you to contact administration. If you're talking about something *at* school, then I take it very seriously. I want to handle this the right way, so I'll contact administration immediately so everything can be reviewed properly."

* * *

Why It Works:

Stays calm, avoids self defense or argument, maintains composure, separates personal and professional boundaries, avoids debate, acknowledges the gravity of the claim, and immediately routes it through official channels, protecting both the teacher and the parent from escalation or missteps.

"I don't want that student sitting next to my child."

You Say:

"I hear you, your child's comfort matters! I'll check what I have observed and to start, we can try a seat change and more supervision. If I notice anything that feels unsafe, I'll take bigger steps to address it and keep you informed along the way."

* * *

Why It Works:

Validates the concern and prioritizes safety without publicly blaming the other child, offers concrete, non escalating actions, and commits to follow up and transparency.

"I'm afraid he will be a school shooter."

You Say:

"Thank you for being transparent with how you're feeling. It must be difficult to say that out loud. Safety is my first priority, so I need to take your concern seriously and make sure the right supports are in place *right away*. I'll involve administration and our support team so your child gets help and we can keep everyone safe."

Note: A teacher must also follow mandated reporting and school safety protocols in this situation: contacting administration, mental health professionals, and possibly law enforcement if imminent risk is suspected.

* * *

Why It Works:

Validates the gravity of the parent's fear, avoids shock or dismissal, and immediately moves the concern into formal safety channels. Balances empathy with mandated action, prioritizing both the child's support and the community's protection.

XII

Special Education and Parent Support

Parents are navigating an exhausting system full of meetings, acronyms, and confusing signals. They don't always know the rules or what's best for their children, but they do want help. By translating, explaining, and collaborating without condescension, you become part of the solution instead of just another gatekeeper.

"I don't understand all of these acronyms."

You Say:

"Thanks for saying that, education does get filled with abbreviations. I'll slow down and explain them clearly so you don't feel left out of the conversation. If any new ones come up, just stop me and I'll translate."

* * *

Why It Works:

Validates the parent's confusion without embarrassment, explains the plan for clarity, and invites ongoing questions to keep communication open.

"They don't listen to me."

You Say:

"That has to be discouraging. We both know kids often test limits with the people they feel safest with. At school, I have seen that both consistency and calm follow through help a lot. Let's share what does work in each setting so your child gets the same message every time."

* * *

Why It Works:

Acknowledges the parent's frustration, sees the behavior as a sign of safety not defiance, and shifts the focus toward consistent strategies that support the child.

"Why can't they read?"

You Say:

"I know how hard it must feel to question this. Reading develops at different paces, and some kids need more time or different strategies. What I can do is show you where your child is right now, what supports we're using, and how together, we can keep building their confidence step by step."

* * *

Why It Works:

Names the parent's frustration without defensiveness, sees reading as a process not a pass/failure activity, and offers concrete direction so the parent feels hope instead of shame.

"He needs an IEP."

You Say:

"I hear you and wanting the right support for him makes sense. An IEP comes through a formal process, but what I can do right now is share what I'm seeing at school and help start that process if you'd like. In the meantime, I'll always use strategies to support him here."

* * *

Why It Works:

Validates the parent's concern, explains the limits of the teacher's role, and offers both immediate support and a concrete path toward evaluation without shutting the parent down.

"I don't know what to do anymore."

You Say:

"I can imagine how heavy that feels. Parenting can be overwhelming, and you don't have to figure it out alone. Let's look at what you've tried, what works, and what types of supports we can put in place so you feel less stuck."

* * *

Why It Works:

Validates the parent's exhaustion, reduces isolation by offering partnership, and shifts the focus toward concrete next steps for support.

"We've tried everything and nothing works."

You Say:

"That sounds exhausting and I can see how much you care about your child. Sometimes it takes a new approach or firm consistency across home and school. Let's look at what's been tried and build a plan together so it doesn't feel like you're carrying this alone."

* * *

Why It Works:

Validates the parent's exhaustion, affirms their effort, and frames the situation from hopelessness to partnership and new possibilities.

"I will spank them/teach them a lesson."

You Say:

"I know you want them to learn from this, but I can't support this type of punishment because my priority is your child's physical and emotional safety. Let's talk about firm, effective alternatives we can use at school and at home so they learn consequences without causing them harm."

* * *

Why It Works:

Sets a clear safety boundary without shaming, preserves the parent's intent to teach, and redirects toward nonviolent, practical strategies and partnership.

"There's nothing wrong with him, it's just excuses."

You Say:

"I hear your perspective. Sometimes what looks like avoidance can actually be a sign of stress, worry, or something deeper. Either way, my goal is to help him develop the skills to face challenges without shutting down. Let's try some strategies and see what makes a difference."

* * *

Why It Works:

Acknowledges the parent's view without arguing, frames behavior as skill-building rather than excuses, and shifts the focus toward practical next steps that support the child.

"He just doesn't listen."

You Say:
"I hear your frustration. Listening can be tough for kids when they feel distracted, overwhelmed, or discouraged. At school, I've found routines they can rely on and small check ins help. Let's continue to share what works in each setting so he feels consistent support."

* * *

Why It Works:
Acknowledges the parent's struggle, examines "not listening" as a skill issue not defiance, and emphasizes consistency and teamwork to support the child.

"She shuts down."

You Say:

"Thank you for telling me, that helps me understand her better. When I see her start to shut down, I'll give her space and check in when she's ready. Together we can find what helps her feel safe enough to jump back in."

* * *

Why It Works:

Acknowledges the parent's insight, treats the behavior as communication rather than defiance, and focuses on emotional safety and partnership to rebuild trust and regulation.

"I don't have time to help him."

You Say:

"I completely understand, life is full, and it's hard to fit everything in. I'll make sure he gets the support he needs here, and I can share small things that take just a few minutes at home to help him keep building confidence."

* * *

Why It Works:

Shows empathy instead of judgment, removes guilt from the parent, and redirects the focus to realistic, manageable ways to support the child's learning.

"I don't know how to help my child with their work."

You Say:

"I know that schoolwork looks different now than when we were kids, and it can feel overwhelming. Remember, you don't have to reteach everything at home. What really helps the most is encouragement, solid routines, and letting *me* know if your child is stuck, and how, so I can give the right supports at school."

* * *

Why It Works:

Acknowledges the parent's insecurity, removes pressure to be the teacher, and frames their role as encourager and partner, reducing stress while keeping the child supported.

"Nobody listens to us."

You Say:

"I'm sorry if you've felt isolated or ignored. I want to make sure your voice is heard here. Let's take time *right now* to go through your concerns together so we can focus on what will best support your child."

* * *

Why It Works:

Validates the parent's sense of being dismissed, shifts the moment into active listening, and views the teacher as an ally who will prioritize their perspective.

"What's wrong with my kid?"

You Say:

"I know it feels overwhelming when things don't go smoothly. There isn't anything 'wrong' with your child. Every student has areas where they struggle and areas where they excel. My job is to figure out the best ways they learn and build on their many strengths."

* * *

Why It Works:

Defuses the negative label, replaces shame with strength based language, and assures the parent that the child is capable and not "wrong," or broken.

"She's gifted."

"She has real strengths and my goal is to always keep her challenged while also supporting the areas where she's still growing. Let's work together to make sure she feels both pushed to reach her potential and supported in that."

* * *

Why It Works:

Affirms the parent's pride, acknowledges the child's abilities, and looks at "gifted" as needing both enrichment and balance, not just acceleration.

XIII

Common Scenarios

When they contact you at crazy hours

You Say:

"I appreciate you reaching out. I can tell you care about your child's progress. I try to keep communication to be within school hours so I can respond thoughtfully. I'll get back to you once I'm back at work and can give your message the attention it deserves."

* * *

Why It Works:

Recognizes the parent's effort, sets a clear communication boundary without sounding dismissive, and reinforces professionalism by emphasizing thoughtful, timely responses.

When a parent adds you on social media

You Say:

"Thanks for reaching out! I keep my social media separate so I can stay focused on school connections in a professional way. I'm always glad to connect with you through email, calls, or school channels whenever you need me."

* * *

Why It Works:

Acknowledges the gesture without shaming, sets a clear boundary in a respectful way, and redirects the relationship back into professional, appropriate spaces.

If you see them hit their child

You Say (in the moment):

"I need to pause here. My role is to keep all students safe, and I can't allow physical discipline on school grounds. Let's step inside and talk through what your child needs so we can work together."

Next Steps:

After the conversation, a teacher must follow mandated reporting laws and school policies. This includes documenting the incident and notifying the appropriate administrator or child protection agency.

* * *

Why It Works:

Immediately grounds the safety boundary, avoids shaming language that could escalate, and redirects toward constructive support. It also positions the teacher as acting from responsibility, not personal judgment.

When a parent wants to discuss in public

You Say:

"Hi! It's nice to see you. Out here I just keep things casual, but I'm always glad to connect more about school when we're back on campus."

* * *

Why It Works:

Keeps the interaction friendly and respectful, sets a boundary so the teacher isn't pulled into a conference in the grocery aisle, and redirects school-related talk to the professional setting.

When a parent won't stop calling

You Say:

"I want to make sure your concerns are heard. Right now, the best way to keep communication clear is to set up a scheduled time to talk, instead of catching calls throughout the day. That way you'll have my full attention, and your child gets the support they need."

* * *

Why It Works:

Acknowledges the parent's persistence as care, sets a professional boundary without shutting them down, and looks at communication as structured and student-focused.

XIV

Parent Archetypes

Every teacher has met them. The helicopter, the apologist, the aggressive, the overwhelmed parents, and more. This section breaks down ten common parent types you'll encounter, what drives their behavior, and how to approach each one without losing your patience or your professionalism.

The Helicopter Parent

Snapshot: Hovers over every assignment, email, and grade, their anxiety about control often comes from love and a fear of their child falling behind.

Approach: Reassure with transparency. Give them a clear plan and defined boundaries so they know things are being handled.

Key Phrase: "You don't have to worry, I've got eyes on it, and here's how you'll know."

The Babying Parent

Snapshot: They see their child as fragile or incapable, stepping in at the first sign of struggle. Their intention is protection, but it blocks growth.

Approach: Validate their care, then gently redirect it toward independence. Emphasize skill building and resilience.

Key Phrase: "You've done a great job supporting! Now let's help them take this next step alone."

The Absent Parent

Snapshot: Hard to reach, inconsistent, or disconnected. Sometimes they're working multiple jobs, sometimes they've just mentally checked out.

Approach: When contact does happen, keep the communication brief, positive, and forward focused. Use these moments of contact to build small trust. Pull the parent in, don't push them away.

Key Phrase: "Here's one quick thing you can do that will really help."

The Aggressive Parent

Snapshot: Comes in hot, loud, defensive, or intimidating. Often masking fear or frustration behind control or anger.

Approach: Stay calm, factual, and professional. Deescalate by naming shared goals and offering clear next steps.

Key Phrase: "Let's both focus on what's best for your child moving forward."

The Victimized Parent

Snapshot: Feels the system, the teacher, or other students are unfairly targeting their child. They seek validation through outrage.

Approach: Acknowledge their frustration, but shift toward partnership and solutions. Keep tone calm and centered on the child's agency.

Key Phrase: "I hear how frustrated you feel. Let's look at what parts we can take control of right now."

The Best Friend Parent

Snapshot: Wants to be *liked* more than *respected* by their child. They blur boundaries and may side with the child even when it undermines you.

Approach: Affirm their relationship while reinforcing that partnership means shared structure. Highlight the importance of consistency.

Key Phrase: "They're so lucky to have a parent who really listens/cares. Let's move towards helping them start to take more responsibility as they grow."

The Overachieving Parent

Snapshot: Everything is a competition such as grades, awards, opportunities. They equate performance with worth and may pressure their child (and you).

Approach: Shift focus from outcomes to growth. Use data and process language to cool their temperature and look at success in a fresh way.

Key Phrase: "The real goal is steady progress, and they're right on track."

The Apologist Parent

Snapshot: Excuses every behavior or low grade, often out of guilt or fear that their child can't handle consequences.

Approach: Show empathy but hold your boundaries. Emphasize natural consequences as opportunities for growth.

Key Phrase: "I understand. Let's keep in mind this is a perfect chance for them to learn."

The Overwhelmed Parent

Snapshot: Trying their best but buried under stress, work, or chaos. Their inconsistency is usually due to exhaustion (or, incompetence, unfortunately), not malice or neglect.

Approach: Offer grace and simplicity. Reduce friction by offering one clear step, one positive note. Show you're on their side!

Key Phrase: "You have a lot on your plate. I will keep this short and sweet. Let me know how I can help here at school."

The Expert Parent

Snapshot: Believes they know more than the teacher or school, often because they once studied teaching/education, work in a school, have read every blog, or listened to every podcast. They mean well but overstep.

Approach: Acknowledge their knowledge and expertise and redirect it toward collaboration instead of control.

Key Phrase: "You clearly know your child very well. Let's combine what you know with what we see here at school to give your child maximum support and consistency."

XV

Templates for Contact

*Use these templates in emails, texts, phone calls, or as a
starter script for in-person meetings. This section gives you
short, flexible templates for every situation from discipline
updates to good news, conference invites, and field trips.
They're designed to save you time while protecting tone and
clarity.*

Positive Behavior Shout Out

Subject: Quick Good News About (Student's Name)!

"Hello (Parent Name),

Just wanted to share a positive note about (Student). They really impressed me today with (specific example, like, helping a classmate, leadership, participation). Please let them know I noticed and appreciated it!

Have a great day,
(Your Name)"

Academic Concern

Subject: Checking In About (Student's Name)'s Progress

"Hi (Parent Name),

I've noticed (Student) has been struggling a bit with (specific subject/skill). I'd love to partner up on some next steps. Maybe we can both encourage (specific habit, like, finishing homework or reviewing notes). I'm confident with a bit of consistency, we'll see improvement quickly.

Warmly,
  (Your Name)"

Discipline Follow Up

Subject: Quick Note About (Student's Name) Today

"Good morning/afternoon, (Parent Name),

I wanted to let you know that (Student) had a brief issue today involving (brief description, like, talking during a lesson/refusing a direction). We talked about it, and they understand what to do differently next time. I just wanted you to hear it directly from me, no major concern, just keeping communication open.

Best,
    (Your Name)"

Missing Assignments/Materials

Subject: Quick Heads Up: Missing Work/Materials for (Student's Name)

"Hello (Parent Name)!

A quick note to let you know (Student) has a few missing assignments/materials in (subject). Nothing major, but I wanted to make sure you were aware so we can get them caught up together. (**Optional**: I'll accept them until Friday for full or partial credit.)

Thanks for your support,
    (Your Name)"

Grade Drop Alert

Subject: Let's Support (Student's Name)'s Progress

"Hi (Parent Name),

I wanted to check in because (Student)'s grade has recently dropped in (subject). I know they are capable of stronger work, and I'd love to see them finish the term strong. Let's touch base on what might help like consistency, tutoring, or a reset plan.

Best,
  (Your Name)"

Invite to Conference

Subject: Scheduling a conference for (Student name)

"Good morning/afternoon, (Parent Name),

I'd like to schedule a quick meeting to discuss (Student)'s progress and goals. Are you available (give two time options)? We can meet in person or virtually, or even on the phone, whichever works best for you.

Thank you,
    (Your Name)"

Field Trip Announcement

Subject: Field Trip Details to (Destination & Date)

"Hello (Parent Name),

We're excited for our upcoming field trip to (destination) on (date). Permission slips are due by (deadline), and students should bring (lunch, jacket, etc.). Please let me know if you're interested in chaperoning, spots are limited but quite appreciated!

Thanks,
   (Your Name)"

Chaperone Request

Subject: Looking for Chaperones for (Trip/Event)

"Hi (Parent Name),

We're looking for a few parent volunteers to help chaperone our (event/trip) on (date). If you're available and interested, please reply by (date). It's always more fun and safer with extra hands on deck!

Best,
  (Your Name)"

Fundraiser Reminder

Subject: (Fundraiser Name) Quick Reminder

"Good morning/afternoon/evening (Parent Name)!

Just a reminder about our (fundraiser name) happening this week. Every bit helps whether you participate, share the link, or just spread the word! Funds go directly toward (specific goal, field trips, classroom supplies, etc.).

Thank you for your support!
  (Your Name)"

Supplies Request

Subject: Quick Classroom Needs

"Hello (Parent Name),

Our class could use a few extra (specific items like tissues, markers, paper towels). If you're able to send any, it's much appreciated but not expected. Thank you for always supporting our classroom community.

Warmly,
    (Your Name)"

End of Term Reminder

Subject: Wrapping Up the Quarter/Semester

"Hi (Parent Name),

As we approach the end of (term), I wanted to remind everyone to double check missing assignments and class projects in (subject). (Student) has been doing well overall, and finishing strong will make a big difference.

Thank you,
  (Your Name)"

Class Update/Newsletter Style

Subject: Quick Classroom Update from (Your Name)

"Hello Families!

Here's a quick look at what's happening in (class name):
   -We're wrapping up (unit/topic).
   -Next week, we'll begin (new topic).
   -Reminders: (any key dates or items).

Thank you for staying connected. I truly appreciate your partnership!
Warmly,
   (Your Name)"

Absent/Missing Student

Subject: Checking In on (Student's Name)

"Good morning/afternoon (Parent Name),

I just wanted to check in since (Student) has been out. I hope everything's okay. When they return, I can help with any missed work or notes, no stress. Please let me know if there's anything you'd like me to send in the meantime.

Best,
(Your Name)"

Appreciation/Partnership Message

Subject: Thank You for Your Support

"Hi (Parent Name)!

I just wanted to take a quick moment to say thank you for your support this year. It truly makes a difference when home and school work together. (Student) benefits so much from your involvement.

Gratefully,
  (Your Name)"

General Response to Concerned Parent

Subject: Re: Your Note About (Student's Name)

"Hello (Parent Name),

Thank you for reaching out. I completely understand your concern about (brief issue, like recent grades, behavior, motivation). I've noticed some of the same things and already have a plan in place to support (Student). I'll keep you updated as we go. I really appreciate you staying involved. It makes a big difference when we work together.

Best,
   (Your Name)"

XVI

Power Phrases

When words fail, this section won't! Here you'll find ready to use phrases that help you take conflict down, build trust back up, and keep communication focused on solutions in both directions. These are the quick lines that help you sound calm, confident, and collaborative, even when things get tense!

Power Phrases

"I can tell you really care about your child's success."

"We're on the same team here."

"Let's figure this out together."

"Thank you for bringing this to my attention."

"I hear what you're saying, and I want to understand more."

"My goal is the same as yours, which is helping your child grow."

"Here's what I've noticed so far."

"I completely understand why you would feel that way."

"Let's focus on what we *can* control right now."

"You know your child best, and I value that perspective."

"Here's what's been working well so far."

"I want your child to feel confident here."

"There's no blame or shame here, we're just looking for solutions."

"I can tell how much effort you're putting in at home."

"You should be so proud of (student)."

"Thank you for trusting me with your child."

"This doesn't have to be perfect, we just want to move forward."

"That's a fair question."

"Here's what I can do on my end."

"Let's come up with a small next step."

"I want to make sure we're communicating in a way that works for you."

"I appreciate how open you're being."

"Let's take the emotion out for a second and look at the data."

"You don't need to handle this alone. We'll give support from school, too."

"Your child has so many strengths, and we're going to build on them."

"I know it's hard to hear, and I'm here to help."

"Here's what progress can look like in the next few weeks."

"Thank you for being proactive about this."

"My door's open to keep the conversation going."

"The goal isn't blame, it's supporting your child."

"(Student) benefits most when we're consistent together."

Add your own below!

XVII

Final Words and Acknowledgments

Responding to Parents (for Teachers)

Final Words

No one gets parent communication right on their first try. It's something you learn slowly one email, one phone call, one tough conference at a time.

In between grading, planning, and everything else that fills your day, these conversations can sneak up and drain you. That's why this book exists: to remind you that every parent interaction is a chance to respond, not react. To protect your peace while protecting the partnership. To lead with calm instead of control.

You don't have to sound perfect or polished. You just have to sound human! Be steady, kind, and clear, because the way we talk to parents shapes the way they see us, and sometimes, the way they see their own child.

Keep using this book. Keep adjusting it. Make it sound like *you*.

And above all, keep showing up for your students, their families, and yourself!

Acknowledgments

To the teachers who stay calm when it would be easier not to, thank you for modeling grace under pressure.

To the parents who show up curious, tired, or nervous but willing to try again, you remind us why this work matters.

To the educators who've ever walked into a parent meeting with their heart pounding and walked out with a little more understanding, this book is for you!

And to everyone reading this between classes, after hours, or during one of *those* weeks. I see you. You're doing work that matters!

About the Author

Chase Nordman spent over a decade in public school classrooms, teaching everything from languages to life skills, and learning just as much from the students as they learned from him. With a Bachelor's degree in Languages and a Master's in Teaching, Chase has studied how people think, speak, and respond. But it wasn't theory that shaped his practice. It was the daily trial and error of real teaching and communicating, where the right words at the right time could change everything.

Now working as a private tutor and certified studio teacher on film and television sets, he has built a career around knowing what people need to hear and how to say it in a way that sticks.

Chase is obsessed with communication, connection, and the craft of teaching. *Responding to Parents (for Teachers)* is his field guide for anyone who works with kids and their parents. It's packed with the kind of language that builds trust, restores focus, and turns hard moments into trust building ones. More than anything, it's about showing up with the words that matter.

Also by Chase Nordman

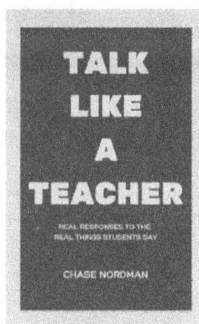

Talk Like a Teacher

Real Responses to the Real Things Students Say! Talk Like a Teacher is the book for all educators with over 150 ready-to-use responses and strategies to tackle the tough things students say and do every day in the classroom. This is the book every educator reaches for when the lesson plan stops and real conversations begin. In classrooms, hallways, and Zoom rooms, students say things that can freeze an adult in their tracks. The words and responses a teacher chooses can build trust or break it. This book supplies those words and responses. Get your copy today and add it to your teacher toolbox.

www.ingramcontent.com/pod-product-compliance
Lightning Source LLC
Chambersburg PA
CBHW051819090426
42736CB00011B/1554